CW01500256

Original title:
Quieted Melts Inside the Mermaid Hale

Author: Kene Elistrand
ISBN HARDBACK: 978-1-80563-337-2
ISBN PAPERBACK: 978-1-80564-858-1

Reflections of the Ocean's Shade

In the soft glow, the tide does wane,
Mirrors of silver, whispers of rain.
Beneath the surface, secrets reside,
In the ocean's cradle, dreams abide.

The moonlight dances on waves so free,
Holding the stories of you and me.
Each crest a memory, each trough a sigh,
In the depths of twilight, our hopes will fly.

Clam Shelters of Secret Thoughts

In the quiet nooks, the clams open wide,
Guarding their treasures, where secrets abide.
Soft whispers echo in the sandy embrace,
Holding the musings of time and space.

Glimmers of thoughts like pearls so rare,
Nestled in shells with delicate care.
Each moment captured, a fleeting glance,
Waiting for tides to stir up a dance.

The Depths of Solitude's Caress

In the depths of night, where shadows blend,
Solitude whispers, a comforting friend.
Holding the burdens of dreams unspoken,
In silence, the heart finds bonds unbroken.

The stillness wraps like a gentle tide,
Cradling wishes we often hide.
Within the abyss, clarity blooms,
In solitude's arms, we shed our glooms.

Twilight Whispers Beneath the Surface

As dusk descends with a soft embrace,
Twilight whispers, a hidden place.
Beneath calm waters, the world recedes,
Swathed in the magic of ancient creeds.

The ocean hums a lullaby sweet,
Drawing us close, with each gentle beat.
In its embrace, the stars ignite,
Guiding the dreamers into the night.

Reveries Underneath the Tide

Beneath the waves where whispers dwell,
The secrets of the ocean swell.
A dance of light, a twinkling spree,
In dreaming depths, we're wild and free.

The currents sing in gentle sighs,
While seafoam drapes the azure skies.
A tapestry of shades unfold,
In oceans deep, both warm and cold.

With every ripple, tales arise,
Of sunken ships and starry skies.
The tide recalls a lullaby,
A serenade where spirits fly.

Lost treasures in the silken sand,
The moonlight's touch, a guiding hand.
In silent caverns, time stands still,
As waves embrace the ocean's will.

So let us dive where wonders gleam,
And weave our thoughts in tidal dream.
For in the depths, our souls shall find,
The magic that the sea entwined.

A Symphony of Shells and Silence

Upon the shore where silence reigns,
The shells conspire in soft refrains.
Each little curve, a story told,
In whispers soft, both shy and bold.

The ocean's pulse, a timeless beat,
In harmony with salty feet.
The breeze carries a gentle song,
Where tranquil echoes hum along.

A conch reveals a hidden sound,
As waves embrace the stony ground.
A symphony of earth and sea,
That dances with integrity.

The silver grains in sunlight play,
Reflecting dreams of yesterday.
In every shell, a memory,
Of tides that kissed our reverie.

So gather close, let nature speak,
In silence soft, we find the sleek.
The ocean's heart beats just for us,
In shells, our secrets lie, we trust.

The Still Waters Hold Their Breath

In twilight's grasp, the waters sigh,
A mirrored world beneath the sky.
The stillness wraps the shore in lace,
As shadows dance with gentle grace.

The stars descend, a twinkling veil,
Reflections weave a mystic tale.
Each ripple still, a thought to ponder,
Where quiet pools invite us under.

With nature's hush, a heartbeat slows,
A tranquil peace that gently flows.
In every breath, a moment lasts,
Where future melds with echoes past.

The moonlight spills like liquid gold,
Over the surface, calm and bold.
In stillness, stories softly gleam,
Like whispers caught in a waking dream.

So linger here, where silence reigns,
And let the stillness ease your pains.
For in the depths, and in the light,
The waters hold their breath each night.

Hidden Murmurs of the Deep

The ocean floor, a world unseen,
Where shadows dance in hues of green.
With every swell, a siren's call,
A symphony beneath it all.

In coral caves where secrets lie,
The whispers of the sea go by.
Each crevice holds a timeless tale,
Of dreams adrift, of ships that sail.

The lanternfish, with flashes bright,
Illuminate the depth of night.
With hidden murmurs, life entwines,
In watery halls, a treasure shines.

With starlit glints, the surface shimmers,
While darkness darts, and mystery glimmers.
Beneath the waves, a heartbeat plays,
As life unfolds in watery ways.

So dive with me where silence breathes,
And share the depths, where nature weaves.
For hidden there, the beauty sleeps,
In murmurs soft, the ocean keeps.

Serenade of Nautical Whispers

In moonlit glow, the waters sigh,
A lullaby, where dreams do lie.
Whispers of salt in the gentle breeze,
Carrying tales of the deep blue seas.

Echoes of ships, long lost in time,
Their secrets held in waves that rhyme.
Stars alight on the ocean's face,
Every ripple a soft embrace.

Beneath the depths, the creatures roam,
Wandering far from their watery home.
The rhythm of life, a dance so free,
In harmony with the vast, deep sea.

Glimmers of silver in twilight's gleam,
Casting shadows where visions dream.
A siren's call, both haunting and clear,
Draws the brave, and whispers near.

Each tide that turns, a verse is spun,
A tale of treasure and battles won.
With every wave, the stories swell,
Of adventures lost, and those who fell.

The Peaceful Call of the Deep

In tranquil depths where silence reigns,
The ocean breathes, a peaceful chain.
Soft currents weave through coral strands,
As secrets drift through ancient hands.

The mermaids sing in voices soft,
Their melodies rise, gently aloft.
Rippling echoes dance on the air,
Carried far, beyond despair.

Bright fish dart in shimmering hues,
Painting the waters with vibrant cues.
Sea turtles glide, a timeless grace,
In the peaceful depths, they find their place.

Sunlight filters through azure waves,
Illuminating the paths of graves.
Lost treasures lie under sand and foam,
In this tranquil realm, they find their home.

A lull of nature, calm and serene,
In the heart of the sea, a world unseen.
The call of the deep, a soothing balm,
Where troubles fade, and souls feel calm.

Silence Beneath the Waves' Dance

Beneath the waves, a quiet dance,
Where time stands still, and dreams entrance.
Bubble-laden whispers softly swell,
In the hush of the sea, all's well.

Slowly swaying, the kelp does bend,
Each motion tells a tale to send.
Through caverns dark, where shadows creep,
A world of silence, secrets keep.

Occasional fish dart, bright as day,
In this realm where colors play.
The moonlight spills, casting glows,
On the hidden life that gently grows.

The great blue expanse, a poet's muse,
In every wave, the heart does choose.
With whispered tales of love and loss,
The silence beneath pays no cost.

The tides may rise, the storms may roar,
Yet in the depths, there's always more.
Life untouched by the world above,
Living in silence, endless love.

Secrets Held in the Depth of the Sea

In the fathomless depths, hidden away,
Whispers of secrets, where shadows play.
The ocean's treasures lie serene,
Guarded by tides, forever green.

Ancient wrecks rest on the sea bed,
Where tales of longing and dreams once tread.
They hold the stories of love and war,
In hushed murmurs, they endlessly implore.

The gentle sway of the rolling tide,
Covers the past where regrets abide.
Anemones bloom in a dance to keep,
The guarded treasures, their secrets deep.

From tangled nets to pearls of light,
Mysteries in darkness, woven tight.
The currents carry a longing song,
To the depths where all secrets belong.

With each ebb, with every flow,
The ocean sings of what we don't know.
In the silence, stories dare to be,
Unfolding softly, beneath the sea.

Gentle Embrace of the Sea Wind

The salty breeze in whispers sings,
Caressing the sands as daylight clings.
Soft echoes dance in the twilight air,
Nature's embrace, tender and rare.

In solitude, the waves confide,
Secrets woven with the afternoon tide.
A fleeting warmth, a soft retreat,
Where the land and sea, in union, meet.

As dusk descends with a velvet hand,
The stars emerge, a jeweled band.
They twinkle down through the misty hue,
A gentle promise of dreams anew.

I feel the pull, a longing deep,
For the ocean's heart, a call to keep.
In every gust, a story flows,
Of distant shores where the wild wind goes.

So let me drift on this breeze tonight,
With the sea as my guide, my heart alight.
In the gentle embrace of the winding sea,
I find my solace; I am truly free.

A Captive Mermaid's Soliloquy

Beneath the waves where shadows play,
I sing my heart, yet none can stay.
A captive of this ocean's keep,
With tears that mingle, dark and deep.

Oh, how I long for the sunlit shore,
To leave this realm forevermore!
Yet here I dwell with dreams untold,
In currents shifting, ancient, bold.

With every tide, a whisper calls,
Through coral halls and moonlit halls.
The sailor's charm, a fleeting hope,
Yet shadows bind, and I cannot cope.

What sailor's heart could comprehend,
The silver songs that twist and bend?
In watery depths, my longing swells,
A lonely tale where silence dwells.

If only fate would let me soar,
To breathe the air and roam the shore.
But here I sing, my heart displayed,
A captive mermaid, forever swayed.

Tranquil Tides in the Moonlit Bay

The moon hangs low in the sultry night,
Bathing the waves in silvery light.
Whispers of peace in the gentle swell,
For in this hour, all is well.

Stars like diamonds kiss the sea,
Each twinkle a secret, wild and free.
Soft lullabies on the ocean's breast,
In this stillness, I find my rest.

With every ripple, a soothing sigh,
The tides converse, as time drifts by.
Carved in the sand, footprints of dreams,
Floating on night's tender beams.

A heron stands by the water's edge,
Guarding the shores, a silent pledge.
This tranquil bay, a sacred space,
Where moments linger, time can't erase.

In the heart of night, all worries cease,
Wrapped in the waves, embraced by peace.
With the moon as my guide, I find my way,
In this harmony, forever stay.

Thoughts Adrift in the Brine

A whisper rolls on the ocean's breath,
Where thoughts adrift find sweet release.
Each wave that crashes tells a tale,
Of lovers lost, of dreams that sail.

Beneath the surface, shadows roam,
In depths where silent thoughts find home.
A lonely buoy, a lighthouse bright,
Guiding the souls through the dead of night.

Salt upon lips, the taste of time,
As seasons shift, the tides sublime.
In currents swirling, my musings flow,
With ebb and tide, as sure as they go.

What secrets lie beneath the foam?
Stories whispered, where sea becomes home.
With each reflection in the briny blue,
Mysteries call, their voices true.

So let my thoughts drift with the tide,
In this vast cosmos, I will abide.
Adrift in dreams, my heart will soar,
Embraced by the sea, forevermore.

Beneath the Shell's Soft Embrace

In the cradle of sand, secrets lie,
Whispers of tides that softly sigh.
Shells gather dreams from the sea's bright heart,
Crafting a world where wonders start.

Moonlit dances on waves that gleam,
Stories entwined in a silvery stream.
Crabs scuttle home in their clever disguise,
Under the watch of the starlit skies.

Each shell a token of journeys untold,
Hiding the treasures of ages old.
Their chambers echo with songs of the deep,
Guarding the secrets they're sworn to keep.

As dusk falls gently, the sea starts to glow,
Guiding lost spirits where soft currents flow.
Embraced by the foam, they drift in delight,
Cradled by waters that shimmer in night.

So linger a while by the ocean's embrace,
Where time stretches thin in the playful chase.
Beneath the shell's hold, forever we'll stay,
In the tender dusk of the close of day.

Murmurs of Enchantment in the Depths

In the shadows where the mermaids sing,
Murmurs from the depths, a magical ring.
Coral palaces beckon, adorned with light,
Bathed in the glow of the moon's silver bite.

Tales of the ancients drift through the sea,
Whispering wisdom, wild and free.
Echoes of laughter, a magical blend,
Calling the lost to discover their friend.

A fish-scaled melody sways through the blue,
Stirring the currents, a dance that's so true.
Reef guardians twirl in a shimmering trance,
Inviting the dreams that in waters prance.

With starfish holding the stories of yore,
Each flick of a tail opens a new door.
As bubbles float up in a sweet ballet,
The depths brim with magic, night fades away.

So heed the charm beneath the waves' crest,
In quiet moments, we find our quest.
Murmurs enchant us to whisper and sway,
In a world where the heart learns to drift, to play.

Hushed Breaths of the Aquatic Realm

Beneath the blue where the shadows blend,
Hushed breaths awaken, secrets transcend.
Fins flicker softly in the gentle tide,
Nurturing dreams as they glide and bide.

Anemones sway in a ballet divine,
Dancing with currents, their elegance fine.
Their colors shimmer through darkness below,
Sharing the wonders of the depths that flow.

Octopuses weave through intricate hide,
Masters of camouflage, clever and sly.
Stealing the light, they emerge with grace,
A riddle of nature, a dance to embrace.

An underwater hush, a world so surreal,
Where even the silence has stories to reveal.
In the heart of the ocean, tranquility reigns,
Binding the sea's song in its gentle chains.

So let us breathe in this vast, soothing breath,
As life intertwines, both in beauty and depth.
In whispers of water, let souls find their place,
In the arms of the ocean's calm, warm embrace.

Serenity Wrapped in Seafoam

On the shore where the horizon meets,
Serenity lingers in soft, gentle beats.
Wrapped in seafoam, the echoes of peace,
Kissing the sands, where worries release.

Seagulls cry out, tales of the air,
While waves curl and bend, a dance so rare.
Each ripple a promise that dreams can unfold,
A soothing caress, a spirit consoled.

The stars twinkle down on the evening's embrace,
Dancing like fireflies lighting the space.
In twilight's glow, the world feels anew,
Serenity beckons, a whisper so true.

In deep blue waters, reflections align,
Painting the heart with a love so divine.
The hush of the sea, a balm for the soul,
Wrapping us gently in its timeless role.

So linger a moment by salt-kissed shore,
Where the heart finds peace, and spirits can soar.
In the sea's tender arms, let troubles depart,
For serenity blooms like a song in the heart.

Whispers of the Ocean's Heart

In the hush of dawn's embrace,
Where waves kiss the sandy shore,
Soft whispers float on the breeze,
Tales of magic and ancient lore.

Beneath the horizon's painted glow,
Secrets of depths unfurl,
Mermaids sing in twilight's flow,
Binding hearts of sea and pearl.

Each tide carries a tale anew,
Of mariners lost to the night,
In the depths where shadows brew,
Hope glimmers, a beacon of light.

The ocean's lullaby calls to dreams,
With every ripple that gleams,
A symphony of ageless flows,
Echoes of joy where magic grows.

In these whispers, we find our way,
To treasures the sea has kept,
For in each note, come what may,
The ocean holds what we've all wept.

Secrets Beneath the Coral Veil

Beneath the waves, a world concealed,
A canvas crafted of vibrant hues,
Corals whisper secrets revealed,
In depths where time forever brews.

Dancing fish in colors bright,
Wreathe among the coral's arms,
In this kingdom, pure delight,
Guarded well by nature's charms.

Lessons lie in silent tales,
Of currents strong and gentle tides,
The ocean's heart forever prevails,
Where mystery and wonder bides.

Lost relics rest on sandy beds,
Stories etched in salt and stone,
With every tide, the past spreads,
Whispers of ghosts who roamed alone.

In this realm where magic swells,
Each coral bloom a spell unspun,
Preserving history that compels,
The ocean's fabric, finely spun.

Tides of Tranquility

When the moonlight dances bright,
Upon the gentle sea's expanse,
A serene calm ignites the night,
Where shadows sway in soft romance.

Waves lap softly at the shore,
Whispering secrets of the day,
In this haven, hearts explore,
Finding peace in nature's sway.

Every ripple speaks of grace,
With echoes of a world so still,
In the ocean's warm embrace,
Time seems to halt at its will.

As stars reflect in liquid glass,
The tides weave dreams both light and deep,
Gentle currents teach us to pass,
Into slumber's arms we leap.

In this moment, joy's unveiled,
The heart opens, fears confined,
Among the waves, our worries sailed,
A tranquil soul forever aligned.

Echoes of a Shimmering Dream

In twilight's glow, the sea does gleam,
With whispers soft, it calls your name,
A place where every soul can dream,
And find the courage to reclaim.

The waves, like stories, rise and fall,
Each crest a vow, each trough a sigh,
In the ocean's depths, we heed the call,
As moonlit paths in silence lie.

Dancing light upon the tide,
Reflecting hopes, a gentle sight,
In shadows, secrets long abide,
While stars above ignite the night.

Each echo carries voices past,
A chorus born of salt and spray,
In dreams we weave, we hold steadfast,
For every heartbeat finds its way.

Awake, arise to morning's kiss,
Let shimmering dreams take to flight,
In ocean's arms, we find our bliss,
For every tide ignites the light.

The Silent Symphony of the Sea

In twilight's glow, the waves do dance,
Whispers of secrets, a hidden chance.
Soft tides gently pull at the shore,
Each crest a story, forevermore.

Moonlight bathes the ocean wide,
As mermaids sing with gentle pride.
Starfish twirl in a silent play,
A symphony woven in shades of gray.

Beneath the surface, life unfolds,
An underwater realm, a treasure to behold.
Coral castles in colors bright,
Guarding dreams through day and night.

Waves weave silver with every sigh,
Casting hopes into the sky.
Echoes of laughter, lost in the foam,
A tranquil heart finds its way home.

The sea's enchantment, a timeless art,
Entwining souls, never to part.
In silence, the symphony calls us near,
A melody sweet, forever clear.

An Aquatic Reverie

In azure depths, the dreams take flight,
Drifting softly in the night.
Glimmers of starlight kiss the waves,
Each ripple a secret the ocean saves.

Bubbles rise like whispers true,
Painting the water in shades anew.
Dancers twirl in fluid grace,
Lost in a never-ending embrace.

Each splash a note in nature's song,
A chorus where we all belong.
Turtles glide with ancient pride,
Through liquid worlds where wonders hide.

Bright fish flash like scattered dreams,
In the depths where magic beams.
Every current tells a tale,
Of underwater storms and gentle gales.

In the silence, we hear the calls,
Where serenity within us sprawls.
As we sink into the depths so free,
We awaken an aquatic reverie.

At Peace with the Underwater World

In tranquil depths where silence reigns,
The heart finds solace, free of chains.
Gentle sways of seaweed fair,
Whispering tales in the cool sea air.

Fish weave patterns in the blue,
Each swirl an echo, alive and true.
Mollusks hide in their quiet shells,
Guarding the stories the ocean tells.

Beneath the surface, fears dissolve,
Embracing the calm as we evolve.
With every breath, the world feels wide,
In the depths where peace does reside.

Echoes of laughter float through the waves,
As the sun dips low, and twilight paves.
We dance with dolphins, free and bold,
In the underwater world where dreams unfold.

Embracing the stillness, a lover's grace,
In the ocean's arms, we find our place.
A gentle tide, a heartbeat slow,
At peace with the water, forever flow.

Liquid Dreams in a Shell

Nestled tight within the sand,
A secret world, both pure and grand.
Soft whispers echo from within,
Where liquid dreams begin to spin.

The ocean cradles them with care,
Lulled by currents, a gentle air.
Shells adorned with colors bright,
Guarding dreams in the soft moonlight.

Tides carry tales from shore to shore,
Of ancient lives who danced before.
In every crevice, a wish is sown,
The magic of water, a love well known.

Whirling visions in the deep,
In hallowed shells where wishes sleep.
Each tide brings forth a brand new start,
Liquid dreams wrapped in nature's heart.

So lend an ear to the ocean's rhyme,
As waves weave stories through the sands of time.
In every shell, a universe felt,
With liquid dreams, our souls are dealt.

Moonlight Over Silent Waters

Beneath the silver glow, so bright,
Lies a world of whispers, pure delight.
Calm waters cradle dreams awoken,
In moonlit magic, words unspoken.

Rippling echoes of the night,
Guide the stars with gentle light.
Softly swaying, the shadows dance,
In this realm, lost in a trance.

The nightingale sings a haunting tune,
While silver beams kiss the lagoon.
Each flicker of light, a promise made,
With the moon above, fears allayed.

In the stillness, secrets reside,
Hidden treasures the waters hide.
A gentle breeze stirs the soul,
In the night's embrace, we feel whole.

So drift with me on this quiet sea,
Where the heart finds peace, and spirits fly free.
For in moonlight's glow, hope is reborn,
In silent waters, we are adorned.

Melodies of the Abyss

In the depths where shadows sway,
Ancient songs weave night and day.
A symphony from the dark below,
Waves of sound in ebb and flow.

Estuary whispers caress the tide,
Where moonlit secrets softly bide.
Echoes linger, a soft refrain,
Calling forth from the ocean's plain.

Chords of silence play their part,
In the ocean's depths, a beating heart.
Bubbles rise like hopes anew,
Sung by creatures in shades of blue.

Underneath the crests and falls,
The sirens weave their mystic calls.
Each note a tale of love and loss,
In the abyss, we bear the cross.

So listen closely to the waves,
To the stories deep culture saves.
For melodies bloom where darkness sings,
In the abyss, the spirit clings.

Soothed by the Aqua Embrace

Gentle waves lap at the shore,
Whispering calm forevermore.
In tranquil moments, hearts align,
Soothed by the water's soft design.

The azure dance under sun's grace,
Inviting laughter, a warm embrace.
Shells and stones, treasures untold,
Stories of wonder, quietly unfold.

Beneath the surface, life abounds,
A hidden world, where joy resounds.
Each ripple cradles dreams anew,
In aqua arms, our spirits flew.

As twilight paints the skies with gold,
Nature wraps us in warmth, behold.
With night's arrival, peace descends,
Amongst the waves, where love transcends.

So let the water guide your way,
To hidden shores where hearts can play.
In aqua embrace, we find our grace,
A sanctuary, our sacred space.

Tranquil Sounds of Distant Shores

Upon the cliff, the seagulls cry,
As whispers of the sea drift by.
Distant shores call to the soul,
Where tides and time gracefully roll.

In the glow of the sunset's blaze,
We find solace, a gentle phase.
Each crash of waves, a lullaby,
Sings of peace under painted sky.

Sands of gold underfoot embrace,
Nature's cadence, a warm trace.
With every breath, the ocean's song,
Guides the weary, where dreams belong.

The horizon melts into shades of blue,
While night unveils its velvet hue.
A serenade of stars brightly gleams,
As we journey forth on woven dreams.

So sit with me on this quiet strand,
Let the ocean weave with the land.
In tranquil sounds, let worries cease,
For in the heart, we find our peace.

Secrets from the Abyss

In shadows deep where whispers dwell,
The ancient tales begin to swell.
A labyrinth where lost dreams fly,
Echoes of time beneath the sky.

The ocean's heart, a hidden door,
Beneath the waves, a world of lore.
In silence dark, the secrets keep,
Guarded by depths where mermaids weep.

With every tide, a story brews,
Of silver fish and tangled hues.
Beneath the moon's soft, watchful eye,
The Abyss whispers its soft sigh.

In coral gardens, colors bright,
The mysteries dance in pale moonlight.
Through ocean's breath, their voices roam,
Secrets of the depths, their home.

Yet in this space of shadows cast,
The echoes fade, the die is cast.
In silence, dreams drift out of sight,
As morning sun unfolds the night.

The Unseen Realm of Tranquility

In a place where silence gloats,
Whispers carry on gentle boats.
Time unfurls in the softest sound,
Where peace is found, and hope is crowned.

The breeze caresses, light, and fair,
With fragrant blossoms, scents to share.
Beneath the boughs of ancient trees,
A realm of calm, a sighing breeze.

In every leaf, a story sways,
Of tranquil nights and sunlit days.
The stars reflect on stillest streams,
Cradling the world in tender dreams.

With each soft step, the heart takes flight,
In realms unseen, the soul ignites.
Boundless wonder, sweet and free,
In tranquil folds of harmony.

Among the whispers, shadows play,
In unseen realms, we find our way.
For in each moment's gentle grace,
Tranquility's warm embrace.

A Ballet of Dune and Tide

In golden sands, where soft winds waltz,
Each grain hides stories, each step, a pulse.
The ocean's hand caresses the land,
In harmony where earth and sea stand.

The wave bows low with a graceful sweep,
A ballet danced in silence deep.
Tides rise high in a rhythmic trance,
While gulls above take their wild chance.

Footprints etch in the shifting shore,
Tales of wanderers, forevermore.
As twilight drapes the world in gold,
Nature's ballet, eternal, bold.

Moonlit nights hold secrets sweet,
Where sand and splash in a lover's greet.
In every pause, in every rise,
Echoes of dreams and lullabies.

Together they move in endless grace,
Dancing to time's unhurried pace.
A ballet of stories, bright and wide,
Of dune and tide, forever tied.

Fantasies in the Shell of the Sea

In perfect shells, the fantasies sleep,
Cradled soft in the ocean's deep.
Whispers of worlds in colors fine,
Echoes of magic, bright, divine.

Each shell a door to dreams untold,
Of mermaid songs and treasures old.
Swirling patterns and whispers sweet,
Lullabies born where sea and sky meet.

With each tide pull, stories race,
In every shell, a hidden place.
Salt-kissed wonders, secrets keep,
In ocean's heart, where silence sleeps.

Children gather with hearts aglow,
Finding dreams in the ebb and flow.
A symphony played by waves so bold,
In the shells of the sea, treasures unfold.

So listen close, and you might hear,
The softest voices drawing near.
In every shell, a wish set free,
A fantasy born in the depths of the sea.

Serene Portraits of Distant Horizons

In the twilight glow, the sky unfurls,
Where dreams take flight and time gently whirls.
Mountains stand guard, their secrets untold,
Casting shadows soft, in hues of gold.

Waves kiss the shore with a silky sigh,
While stars awaken in the velvet sky.
Each breath a promise of journeys anew,
Painted in colors of azure and dew.

The whispering winds wrap the earth in peace,
Where troubles fade and the heart finds ease.
In gilded moments, the world feels right,
As horizon and soul dance in soft light.

With every glance, the vistas unfold,
Stories of wonders in silence retold.
Embraced by nature, a love so profound,
In serene portraits, solace is found.

Beneath the expanse, time flickers and flies,
In the tender embrace of endless skies.
As twilight lingers, our spirits will soar,
To distant horizons, forevermore.

The Calm Within the Maelstrom

In the heart of the storm, where chaos reigns,
A stillness resides that quietly gains.
Beneath every wave that wildly thrashes,
Lies a calm embrace where no fear clashes.

Lightning may dance in a tempestuous show,
Yet deep in the waters, the soft currents flow.
With every clash, there's a beat that stays,
A rhythm unbroken through tempest's frays.

The eye of the cyclone, a wondrous sight,
Where peace wraps the world in velvet delight.
While winds howl and rage, one can learn to breathe,
In the core of confusion, the heart finds reprieve.

Against the dark tumult, the soul takes its stand,
Steady and strong, like a castle of sand.
In turmoil's embrace, we find our way home,
Woven in strength, never destined to roam.

So dance in the fury, rejoice in the plight,
For after the tempest will come dawn's light.
Within every storm, we uncover a truth,
That calm resides deep, forever our root.

Veils of Silence Over Silver Shores

In the hush of the night, the waters gleam bright,
Veils of silence weave through the moon's gentle light.
Soft whispers of waves caress pebbled sands,
As stars stitch the heavens with luminous hands.

A lullaby echoes where sea meets the sky,
As night drapes her coat, and soft breezes sigh.
The silvered shores hold a magic divine,
In moments like these, our spirits entwine.

Crickets sing softly, joining the tide,
As dreams dance unbidden on currents that ride.
Each heartbeat a promise in shadowed embrace,
Where peace in the darkness leaves no single trace.

Lavender skies give way to the dawn,
With hues brushing edges of night gently drawn.
In silence, the shore whispers tales of old,
With secrets held dearly, and stories retold.

So wander the beaches where night meets the day,
In veils spun of whispers, where moments won't stray.
For silver shores cradle the heart's gentle yearn,
In soft silences, we find what we learn.

A Whisper In the Ocean's Cradle

A whisper drifts softly over the tide,
Where secrets are buried and dreams come alive.
In the ocean's embrace, all worries dissolve,
As nature's sweet chorus helps hearts to evolve.

The waves paint a canvas of frothy delight,
Each crest a reflection of stars shining bright.
With moonlight as painter, the world softly glows,
In whispers of waters, tranquility flows.

Shells murmur stories of long-lost design,
With each ebb and flow, their secrets align.
Beneath the blue depths, where shadows do graze,
The ocean cradles our thoughts in her waves.

The sun kisses horizon, a warm golden hue,
In rippling waters, our hearts feel anew.
Those whispers, gentle, guide us back home,
Where in love we will gather, no longer to roam.

So listen, dear traveler, to the sea's gentle plea,
For whispers in cradles hold wisdom set free.
In the symphony's swell, let your spirit rejoice,
In the ocean's vast cradle, embrace your own voice.

The Stillness Between the Currents

In twilight's grasp, the river flows,
Where whispers dance and silence glows.
Beneath the boughs of dreaming trees,
The heart finds peace, the soul's unease.

Ripples weave a tapestry,
Of ancient tales and mystery.
The gentle sway, the quiet murmur,
In tranquil dreams, our thoughts simmer.

A moment hangs, as time stands still,
In nature's hand, we find our will.
As shadows blend with fading light,
We chase the stars into the night.

The currents speak of journeys vast,
Of futures bright and shadows cast.
In stillness lies a secret song,
A melody where hearts belong.

So linger here, where thoughts unwind,
In flowing peace, true love we find.
The stillness holds, forever waits,
A tender dance that fate creates.

A Solstice of Starlit Seas

Upon the shore where starlight gleams,
The ocean mirrors our wild dreams.
With every wave, a tale is spun,
A dance of light, where night is won.

The moon bestows her silver glow,
Upon the tides that ebb and flow.
In whispered winds, the secrets stir,
As hearts unite with every purr.

The vast expanse, where wishes soar,
And sails are filled with tales of lore.
In solstice nights, the heavens beam,
As hope awakens, bright as a dream.

Embrace the night, let spirits soar,
The starlit sea, forevermore.
With laughter woven through the air,
We find our joy, our hearts laid bare.

So gather close, and feel the breeze,
In harmony with starlit seas.
For magic lies in every wave,
In every heart that love will save.

Glistening Reflections of Underwater Dreams

Beneath the waves, where wonders gleam,
The world awakens, lost in dream.
The corals sway like dancers' grace,
In hidden realms, a sacred space.

Glistening fish in colors bright,
Paint underwater canvases of light.
With every swirl, a tale unfolds,
Of ancient mariners and their golds.

Each bubble carries whispers soft,
Of sunken treasures, lost aloft.
In tranquil depths, we roam and glide,
In the embrace of the ocean's tide.

Through briny depths, our spirits flow,
With every pulse, the wild winds blow.
In shimmering hues, we find our way,
In underwater dreams where dolphins play.

So dive into the mystic blue,
And let the currents carry you.
For in this realm, we learn to trust,
To find our dreams, as all dreams must.

Slumber in the Depths of the Blue

In the embrace of ocean's deep,
Where gentle whispers lull to sleep.
The world above fades out of sight,
While dreams unfurl in silent night.

With every wave, a heartbeat sighs,
Beneath the surface, secrets lie.
In tranquil shadows, spirits dwell,
Where time stands still, and stories swell.

The moon casts spells on waters wide,
As creatures dance, their hearts our guide.
In velvet dark, we drift away,
To find the peace of night's ballet.

So sink into the mystic sea,
Let go of all, and simply be.
In slumber's hold, we find our grace,
In depths of blue, our rightful place.

Awake reborn, as dreams unfold,
With whispers sweet, both brave and bold.
In every tide, we find our way,
In slumber's heart, forever stay.

Beneath the Serene Wave

In stillness where the shadows play,
A world beneath the gentle sway.
Whispers of secrets, soft and low,
In tranquil depths, where time moves slow.

Dancing lights in waters deep,
Where coral gardens secrets keep.
Each fleeting glance, a tale unfolds,
Of ancient myths and treasures gold.

The rhythm of the ocean's breath,
Awakens life, yet hushes death.
In unity, the currents breeze,
A silent song beneath the seas.

Fish glide like thoughts on quiet streams,
Echoes of long-forgotten dreams.
A ballet to the moon's bright gaze,
In the heart of the ocean's maze.

As twilight falls, the shadows blend,
In waters deep, where journeys end.
Beneath the serene wave, I find,
The stillness soothes the restless mind.

The Subdued Song of the Reef

Upon the crest of sapphire blue,
Where lullabies of gales renew.
The reef calls gently, soft and clear,
In every tide, a voice we hear.

Through coats of coral, life will weave,
A tapestry where dreams believe.
Each creature sings in muted hue,
A symphony of life, anew.

Glimmers of hope in salty air,
And gentle waves with whispered prayer.
In layers deep, the harmony,
Unfolds the fragility of glee.

The ocean's pulse, a steady guide,
In currents strong, we trust and bide.
With patience borne from ages past,
We seek the beauty that will last.

To linger here is to embrace,
The subtle breath of ocean's grace.
The subdued song of the reef calls loud,
A serenade to nature's crowd.

Unseen Currents

In waters dark, where few have tread,
The whispers of the deep, unsaid.
A dance of currents, swift and sly,
Beneath the surface, secrets lie.

Silent eddies, weaving dreams,
Glimmers flash like fleeting beams.
They twist and twirl, a hidden threat,
In realms where fears and hopes are met.

Yet in this chaos, beauty thrives,
With every pulse, the ocean jives.
A hidden world, so rich, serene,
In unseen currents, calm and keen.

Not all that stirs can bring despair,
For in the depths, there's joy to share.
The flowing tides, both fierce and kind,
Reveal the magic, intertwined.

To sail the waves, embark, be bold,
Through unseen currents, stories told.
Each splash an echo, wild and true,
In currents' arms, we start anew.

The Stillness of Sunlit Depths

Beneath the sun, where light descends,
The stillness whispers, time suspends.
In golden shafts, the water glows,
A world of peace, where stillness flows.

Each bubble rises, laughter light,
A dance of grace, a pure delight.
The gentle sway of seaweed bends,
In harmony, the ocean blends.

Within this realm of radiant hue,
The heart finds solace, old yet new.
While laughter echoes through the blue,
Each moment blooms, a wondrous view.

The sunlit depths, a sacred space,
In quietude, we find our place.
With every breath, the waters sing,
To nature's peace, our hearts take wing.

In stillness, souls will drift and sway,
Embraced by love in ocean's play.
The beauty of the sunlit sea,
Reflects the calm that sets us free.

The Lament of the Ocean's Deep

In shadows deep, where secrets hide,
The ocean whispers, a mournful tide.
With waves that sigh, and currents weep,
The heart of the sea shall ever keep.

Ancient tales in every swell,
A song of sorrow, a timeless bell.
For each lost sailor, a spirit's plea,
Entwined forever with memory.

Beneath the foam, a world of tears,
Where dreams of light dissolve in fears.
Yet beauty cradled in each dark wave,
A silent promise, the bold and brave.

The stars above, a distant guide,
To navigate through the ocean's pride.
With hearts that ache and voices low,
The ocean's deep, eternal flow.

The cry of gulls, the wind's lament,
Echoes of souls, a life well spent.
As tides retreat, a soft embrace,
For every heart, a sacred space.

A Dreamer's Refuge Beneath the Waves

Beneath the swell, where dreams take flight,
A refuge found in the velvet night.
With coral beds that cradle the lost,
And memories drifting, no matter the cost.

In gentle hush, the currents weave,
A tapestry rich, for those who believe.
A world alive with vibrant hues,
Where every shade tells tales anew.

The dance of fish, a silent waltz,
Timeless grace, with no faults.
In this haven, the dreamers hide,
Among the wonders, they choose to bide.

Whispers of magic in ripples sound,
A promise whispered, all around.
As bubbles rise like hopes released,
In this embrace, the heart finds peace.

Glimmers of light through water's veil,
A soothing hymn in a sailor's tale.
The depths below, a world to explore,
A dreamer's refuge, forevermore.

Silent Breeze Through Coral Kisses

In the ocean's breath, a whisper flows,
A silent breeze where the coral grows.
Through arches bright, the shadows play,
In vibrant hues, the dreams drift away.

With every wave, a tender grace,
An embrace softens time and space.
Where ripples break against the shore,
And secrets linger forevermore.

The ballet of tides, a gentle tune,
Dancing softly beneath the moon.
The coral crowns in sapphire sea,
Where nature sings of harmony.

In hidden nooks, the colors blend,
A symphony sweet that will not end.
With each caress of the ocean's breath,
A vibrant pulse beyond mere death.

The silent breeze, a lover's sigh,
In the depths, where dreams never die.
Through coral kisses, the heart is healed,
In the ocean's arms, all truth revealed.

Hidden Harmonies of the Deep

In depths unknown, the silence thrums,
With hidden harmonies, the ocean hums.
The secrets sung in liquid tones,
A symphony played on ancient stones.

With every tide, a note is cast,
A fleeting echo of the past.
Where shadows dance in softest light,
And the world above fades out of sight.

Among the waves, where wonders dwell,
The siren's call a gentle spell.
With melodies that lift and weave,
A tapestry born for those who believe.

In midnight's grip, the ocean sleeps,
Guarding the dreams that the darkness keeps.
Through gentle swells, the wisdom flows,
In hidden depths, the heart still knows.

A serenade of peace unfolds,
In whispered tones, the ocean holds.
A harmony rich as starlit skies,
With hidden truths, the soul will rise.

The Calm of Tideless Seas

In twilight's glow, the waters gleam,
A hush descends, a gentle dream.
The moonbeams dance on silent tides,
Where shadows linger, calm abides.

No storm to break the perfect night,
Just stars above, a soothing light.
The world slows down, the heart finds peace,
In this stillness, troubles cease.

With every wave, a whispered sigh,
As time drifts softly, passing by.
In tranquil depths, the secrets lie,
The quiet speaks, the winds reply.

From distant shores, the breezes come,
Carrying tales of waves and sun.
With every breath, we weave our fate,
In waters warm, we contemplate.

A haven found in nature's grasp,
Where life's demands feel light as glass.
Embraced by calm, we yearn to stay,
In tideless seas, our worries sway.

Secrets Cradled by Tidal Waves

Beneath the surf, the secrets hum,
In watery caves where shadows come.
The tides embrace with gentle grace,
Guarding whispers of a hidden place.

With each swell, a story flows,
Of mariners lost, the ocean knows.
A symphony of salt and sand,
Written by waves upon the strand.

In swirling depths, the dreams are kept,
Where echoes of the past have wept.
These mysteries held in brine so deep,
Awake at night when others sleep.

The siren's call through silent night,
Entwines the hearts with pure delight.
As foam meets shore, they weave their yarn,
Of beauty found and tales that charn.

A fleeting glance at visions bright,
Dissolved by dawn's retreating light.
Yet still they linger, forever bound,
In tidal waves, where dreams are found.

Chronicles Beneath the Seafoam

In frothy waves, the legends swell,
Chronicles told where mermaids dwell.
Among the reefs, the tales entwine,
Of heroes brave and ghosts that shine.

Each bubble bursts with stories old,
Of sunken ships and treasures bold.
Beneath the surface, whispers glide,
In seafoam's embrace, where secrets hide.

The currents weave a tapestry,
Of life beneath the endless sea.
With every roll, a page is turned,
And ancient dreams are softly burned.

In salty air, the echoes call,
Of distant lands, where mermaids sprawl.
Their laughter sings in ocean's breath,
A vibrant hymn, defying death.

So listen close as waters churn,
For in each wave, there's much to learn.
An age-old tale of life once spun,
In seafoam's cradle, we are one.

Whispers of the Ocean's Cradle

In the ocean's cradle, whispers weave,
Secrets carried on the breeze.
The lullaby of salt and spray,
A soothing balm at end of day.

With every splash, a soft refrain,
Echoes of joy, or even pain.
They linger long, a soothing sound,
In nature's arms, our hearts are found.

Beneath the waves, a world alive,
With creatures dancing, they survive.
A silent story flows through brine,
Where life and magic intertwine.

The tides will speak, if ears are clear,
Of whispered vows, of love sincere.
As moonlight kisses ocean deep,
In stillness, promise finds its keep.

A treasure trove of history,
In every wave, a mystery.
So let us linger, hearts entwined,
In whispers soft, our souls aligned.

Enchanted Waters of Stillness

In the hush of twilight's grace,
Ripples dance on reflection's face.
Moonlight weaves a silver thread,
Whispers of secrets softly spread.

Beneath the quiet, shadows sway,
Where dreams and reality softly lay.
The world fades out, a tapestry spun,
In the embrace of the night, all is one.

Veils of mist in gentle embrace,
Cradle the shores, a soft, warm place.
Each droplet carries tales untold,
Mapped over ages, in silence bold.

Through shallow depths, the echoes wail,
A call to hearts, an ancient tale.
Each splash a memory, lost, anew,
In enchanted waters, they drift through.

Glancing stars on the water's crest,
Invite the weary soul to rest.
Underneath the stillness, hearts find flight,
In the enchanted waters of the night.

The Weight of Water's Silence

The moon hangs low, a sentinel bright,
Guarding stillness with its quiet light.
Each wave a whisper, a lullaby's tune,
Bearing the weight of dreams, like a balloon.

Within the depths, shadows combine,
Mysteries linger, artfully entwined.
Nature's breath pauses, bid time to still,
In the vast water's arms, we find our will.

Secrets, unspoken, ripple below,
Bound by silence, where few dare to go.
The weight of water knows every sigh,
Each heart's heavy burden, and reason why.

As starlight flickers on the surface fair,
A tapestry woven with delicate care.
In the quietude, we find our strength,
Awakening whispers, revealing their length.

Embraced by water's gentle fold,
An echo of stories, waiting to be told.
In silence profound, we learn to soar,
The weight of water beckons us more.

Veils of Oceanic Dreams

Beyond the waves, where visions bloom,
Lies a world stitched with silken gloom.
Veils of azure and lullabies blend,
An oceanic dreamscape where time bends.

Seashells glisten like treasures sought,
Harboring secrets in every thought.
They sing softly of shores long past,
Of journeys taken, shadows cast.

The tide whispers tales of what's to come,
In echoes of surf, a rhythmic drum.
Each ebb and flow, a heartbeat's refrain,
An endless cycle, joy mingled with pain.

Beneath the surface, colors collide,
Where fish weave stories of the deep tide.
In veils of mist, the dreams come alive,
Oceanic wonders, where spirits thrive.

With every wave, a promise is made,
In the heart of the ocean, dreams never fade.
Here in these waters, the world holds its breath,
Veils of oceanic dreams dance with death.

Undercurrents of Solitary Beauty

In the depths where the light dares not tread,
Lies beauty untouched, where many fear to spread.
Each current flows with grace and might,
Undercurrents weaving shadows from light.

A silent ballet, the sea creatures twirl,
In a world unseen, where mysteries whirl.
Their beauty profound, in hushed serenade,
In solitude's arms, a spectacle made.

Coral castles rise, vibrant and bold,
Guarding the quiet where stories unfold.
Each grain of sand, a history penned,
In the embrace of the waves, that never end.

The ocean hums a timeless song,
Where solitary beings gracefully belong.
In every bubble, in every swirl,
Lies a whisper of life, a wondrous unfurl.

In the hush of solitude, unity brims,
With the essence of life that forever swims.
In the depths lies beauty, raw and true,
Undercurrents guiding dreams as they renew.

The Siren's Subtle Reverie

In twilight's glow, the whispers weave,
A melody that hearts believe.
With gentle tides, the secrets swell,
The siren sings her silent spell.

Beneath the waves, where dreams may dwell,
Lies tales of love too sweet to tell.
With every note, the waters sigh,
And stars above begin to fly.

Her voice, a balm for weary souls,
Entwines with currents, softly rolls.
Each haunting phrase, a soft embrace,
A call to join the ocean's grace.

Yet shadows lurk beneath the crest,
Where laughter fades and sorrows rest.
For every heart that longs to drift,
Shall find the depths both strange and swift.

So heed her song and tread with care,
For beauty hides in depths of air.
The siren's dream, a haunting chime,
Awaits the brave, both yours and mine.

Shadows in the Sunlit Cove

In sunlit nooks, where shadows play,
The whispers dance in bright array.
Among the rocks, where secrets hide,
Dreams echo soft, like a tranquil tide.

The sea breeze carries tales of yore,
Of brave adventurers on the shore.
Each wave that crashes, a story spins,
Of battles lost, of hearts that win.

Yet in the light, dark edges creep,
Beneath the joy, there's sorrow deep.
For every spark that warms the day,
A shadow lingers, fades away.

With laughter bright and sun's warm hue,
The cove's embrace feels fresh and new.
But heed the love, both near and far,
For shadows shift beneath the star.

So wander here, but know the dance,
Of light and dark in fate's own trance.
In every gleam, a shade shall lie,
In Sunlit Cove, both laugh and cry.

Flickers of Stillness in Deep Waters

In silent depths, the stillness gleams,
A world alive with whispered dreams.
Each flicker soft, a story spun,
Of time unbound, of battles won.

The surface calm, like glass so clear,
Hides mysteries that nature holds dear.
With every ripple, a voice calls out,
From shadows deep, where fears may flout.

Fish dart past, like arrows fleet,
In the deep blue, their heartbeats greet.
With every pulse, life ebbs and flows,
In hidden realms where nobody knows.

Yet silence speaks in quiet tones,
A language formed from ancient stones.
As currents draw the mind to rest,
The heart finds peace, a fleeting quest.

In deep waters, where thoughts collide,
The flickers dance, forever bide.
For stillness holds a secret key,
To endless realms beneath the sea.

The Tranquil Heart of the Sea

In azure depths, a calm prevails,
A tranquil heart, where silence sails.
The waves, like whispers, softly sigh,
Beneath the vast and watchful sky.

With every pulse, the ocean breathes,
As time unfurls its liquid leaves.
A world of blue, both pure and wide,
Holds treasures deep, where dreams abide.

The lull of tides, a soothing sound,
In rhythm's march, we are unbound.
Each ebb and flow, a tender kiss,
A moment's peace, a fleeting bliss.

Yet storms may rise from tranquil seas,
With fury borne on tempests' breeze.
But in the calm, there lies a grace,
Where every soul can find their place.

So seek the heart where stillness reigns,
Beyond the depths, past hidden chains.
For in the sea, both wild and free,
Lies tranquil hope, eternally.

Sibilant Secrets of the Sea

Whispers in the wind do play,
Dancing with the salt and spray.
Mysteries wrapped in foam and tides,
Where the ancient ocean hides.

Echoes of the lost, the found,
Stories in each wave, profound.
A tapestry of dreams once spun,
In the depths where shadows run.

Secrets bind the twilight breeze,
In the ripples, knowledge flees.
Sea creatures waltz in endless chime,
Guarding ageless tales of time.

Beneath the moon's soft, silken gaze,
Fractured light in ocean haze.
Listen close to what they say,
In the ocean's sibilant sway.

Soft Echoes of Ancient Waters

In the depths where silence reigns,
Drifting thoughts like smoky chains.
Muffled echoes, calling deep,
In the shadows where secrets sleep.

Waves embrace the pebbled shore,
Singing songs of days of yore.
Rippling tales of joy and woe,
As the ages ebb and flow.

Crystal currents weave the dream,
Mirrored silvers, soft and gleam.
Each droplet holds a memory,
Whispers of the endless sea.

In twilight's arms, whispers twine,
Ancient wisdom, pure and fine.
A gentle heart that never weeps,
In the waters, time softly creeps.

Murmured Motions of the Deep Blue

Beneath the tides where shadows play,
Murmurs drift in soft ballet.
Gentle sighs in currents glide,
Whispers of the ocean wide.

Each swell, a story softly told,
Through deeps where wonders unfold.
Beneath the waves, life thrums and beats,
In harmony, the ocean greets.

Tangled dreams in kelp entwined,
Seekers of the lost, resigned.
In hidden places where they roam,
The sea becomes a client home.

Hushed vibrations stir the night,
As moonbeams dance in silver light.
In every splash, a past unfolds,
Mysteries the ocean holds.

A Hidden Sanctuary Among the Waves

In a cove where whispers blend,
Time suspends, as dreams commend.
Sheltered from the world's harsh glare,
A sanctuary, fine and rare.

Secrets bloom like coral bright,
Guarded by the stars at night.
The ocean breathes, a sacred hymn,
In twilight's glow, the lights grow dim.

Here the heart can find its peace,
A tender pause, a sweet release.
Sirens call with voices strong,
Inviting you to drift along.

In every tide that ebbs and flows,
A gentle warmth, the ocean knows.
Within its depths, we find our grace,
In hidden sanctuary's embrace.

A Lullaby for Lost Souls

Close your eyes, dear wandering heart,
The moon whispers songs from afar.
In the night, dreams softly start,
Guiding you home where you are.

Stars will cradle your weary flight,
Bathed in silver, a gentle glow.
Rest in peace beneath the night,
For lost souls find solace below.

Winds may wail, and shadows weep,
Yet here in twilight, you shall stay.
In the silence, secrets keep,
Till dawn arrives to light the way.

Take my hand, for you are not alone,
In this realm of dreams, we'll find.
With each breath, a new tone,
Binding the weary with the kind.

Drift in whispers, soft as lace,
Cradled in the night's embrace.
In this lullaby's warm grace,
May you find your rightful place.

Reflections in the Coral Mirror

Beneath the waves, the colors dance,
In a world where shadows play.
Each ripple holds a fleeting chance,
To glimpse the dreams of yesterday.

Coral blooms in fiery hues,
With secrets twined in its embrace.
In tranquil depths, we brush away blues,
Finding truths time cannot erase.

Fish dart like whispers through the blue,
Tracing patterns of what can be.
In the mirror of the ocean's view,
Lies the past, a painted sea.

Listen close, the ocean speaks,
Each wave a tale of loss and love.
Through the depths, the silent seeks,
For stories woven from above.

Reflecting hopes, like shards of glass,
In the coral depths, soft yet bold.
In tides of time, we learn at last,
The treasures that the sea once told.

Shadows of the Deep

In the dark where secrets lie,
Beneath the waves, shadows roam.
Echoes whisper, and creatures sigh,
In the deep, they seek a home.

Flickering light of bioluminescence,
Draws the curious, bold and brave.
Here, in silence, exists a presence,
That tells of journeys through the wave.

Ancient spirits drift alone,
Carried by currents' gentle flow.
In their depths, memories are sewn,
Of lost sailors and tales of woe.

Through the abyss, a path unfolds,
In the depths, hope quietly stirs.
Stories of love and legends told,
Mix with silence when the ocean purrs.

Under the stars, shadows entwine,
Weaving a tapestry of lore.
In the stillness, always divine,
The shadows dance forevermore.

The Gentle Caress of Saltwater

Feel the kiss of the ocean breeze,
As it whispers soft in your ear.
With each wave, the world finds ease,
Calm and soothing, ever near.

Saltwater's embrace is a tender balm,
Healing hearts with whispers sweet.
In the chaos, find the calm,
A place where water and spirit meet.

Waves roll in with a gentle sigh,
Bringing tales from the distant shore.
Beneath the skies, our spirits fly,
On currents, we long to explore.

The sun reflects on the tranquil sea,
A shimmering path of golden light.
In the salt, find your jubilee,
And dance with the waves into the night.

Hear the laughter within the foam,
A song of freedom softly sung.
In its rhythm, feel at home,
The caress of saltwater, forever young.

Secrets Beneath the Silver Waves

In depths where sunbeams barely gleam,
The whispers weave a timeless dream.
With shadows dancing on the sand,
Secrets dwell in ocean's hand.

Mermaids hum of ancient spells,
Luring sailors—cast in wells.
With every crest and gentle fall,
The ocean sings to one and all.

In shipwrecks old, the stories sleep,
While tides keep vigil, dark and deep.
Their tales of love, their cries of woe,
Are carried where the wild winds blow.

A pearl of wisdom, lost yet found,
In every wave, a truth unbound.
The sea keeps watch, a knowing guide,
For hearts who dare to dream and bide.

So listen close and heed the call,
The silver waves embrace us all.
For within their depths, though far away,
Lie secrets waiting, night and day.

Dreams in a Coral Sanctuary

In gardens bright where colors sing,
The coral blooms and soft fins spring.
A secret world beneath the tide,
Where whispered dreams in currents ride.

The anemones sway in time,
To tunes of the ocean—pure and prime.
With fish that flit like thoughts set free,
Their laughter ripples through the sea.

A sea turtle glides, ancient and wise,
Through coral arches to the skies.
With every stroke a story told,
Of journeys vast and treasures bold.

Seahorses dance in colorful veil,
While starfish glitter like legends pale.
Each creature holds a vision bright,
In coral dreams of day and night.

So wander where the waters twirl,
In this sanctuary, watch life unfurl.
For here in the arms of the sea,
Our dreams embrace eternity.

Lullabies in the Tidepool

In tidepools shallow, soft and clear,
Nature sings a lullaby near.
The crabs scuttle, the barnacles cling,
To rhythms of waves that gently sing.

Each ripple holds a tender tune,
A serenade sung to the moon.
With shells as drums in a breezy play,
Lullabies weave through end of day.

Starfish twinkle with sleepy eyes,
While seaweed brushes beneath the skies.
The whispered sighs of ocean's breath,
Are promises whispered beyond death.

In twilight's glow, reflections gleam,
As nature cradles all in dream.
With each soft splash and dip of tide,
In lullabies, our hearts abide.

So close your eyes, heed the call,
Where tidepools wait to cradle all.
For here in the gentle ebb and flow,
The world finds rest in the afterglow.

Echoes of a Gentle Abyss

In silence deep, where darkness sways,
The echoes hum of forgotten days.
With gentle currents weaving by,
The abyss whispers a lullaby.

Ghostly shadows glimmer faint,
Of stories worn, a sailor's plaint.
In caverns vast, where time stands still,
The heartbeats pause, yet dreams fulfill.

A dolphin's call breaks through the dark,
A flicker of life, a hopeful spark.
In watery realms where secrets dwell,
The abyss holds wonders only time can tell.

From shipwrecked souls to coral shrines,
Each echo carries threads of lines.
In whispered tones of love and strife,
The sea reveals the pulse of life.

So dive deep where the shadows play,
Embrace the echoes that drift away.
For in the gentle pull of the tide,
Lies the abyss, where dreams confide.

The Hushed Dance of the Sea Nymph

In twilight's glow, the waters gleam,
Where shadows swirl in silver stream.
A nymph with hair of kelp and pearl,
Dances softly, secrets unfurl.

She twirls with grace, a whispered sigh,
Beneath the waves where wonders lie.
Her laughter mingles with the tide,
As moonlit dreams begin to glide.

In coral groves, her song takes flight,
Through hidden realms of sheer delight.
A shimmer here, a flicker shown,
The ocean's heart, her dance, her own.

Time stands still, the world falls bare,
Lost in her spell, a silent prayer.
With every move, the currents beckon,
The sea's embrace, a blessed reckoning.

So join her dance, let worries cease,
In ocean's arms, you'll find your peace.
The hushed nymph spins, beneath the hue,
In waters deep, your spirit renew.

Lullabies of the Deep Blue

Softly now the ocean sings,
A lullaby on gentle wings.
With every wave, a whispered tune,
Beneath the watchful, silver moon.

Tales of sailors lost at sea,
Dreams of mermaids, wild and free.
The rhythm of the tides unfurls,
As starlit dreams embrace the pearls.

In caverns deep where shadows play,
The lullabies will guide the way.
With every note, the waters sway,
A promise of a brighter day.

Close your eyes and drift away,
The ocean's heart will gently sway.
In twilight's hush, let troubles cease,
For in its depths, there lies pure peace.

So listen close, let magic weave,
In the deep blue, you'll believe.
For every heart that dares to roam,
The lullabies will lead you home.

Echoing the Siren's Call

Upon the rocks, where shadows play,
A siren sings the night away.
Her voice, a haunting, sweet embrace,
Calls forth the sailors to her grace.

Echoes drift on windswept air,
With every note, a spell laid bare.
Entranced they sail toward the shore,
Where dreams and dangers intertwine once more.

Beneath the waves, where secrets thrum,
The siren's song, a soft, sweet hum.
With every breath, the waters swell,
As night unfolds its ancient spell.

Yet caution urges, hearts must fight,
For beauty hides in darkest night.
Not all who follow find their way,
In siren's arms, some choose to stay.

So heed the song, but stay afloat,
Lest you be caught in love's true coat.
The echoing call, both fierce and sweet,
Awaits the hearts it dares to meet.

The Quiet Depths of Enchantment

In quiet depths where shadows dwell,
A world concealed, a whispered spell.
The currents weave a tale untold,
Of magic deep and treasures bold.

A kingdom waits beneath the waves,
Where light and dark in silence crave.
The coral castles, soft embrace,
Hold secrets of this hidden place.

The gentle crunch of ocean's kiss,
An echo of forgotten bliss.
As time unwinds its silken thread,
In tranquil blue, all fears are shed.

So delve within, where wonder flows,
And find the peace that stillness knows.
In every ripple, life's refrain,
The quiet depths call you again.

Embrace the calm, let worries drift,
In ocean's arms, you'll find your gift.
The depths enchant, their magic spun,
In quiet worlds where dreams are won.

Resting in a Sea of Tranquility

In whispers soft, the waters sway,
A lullaby for night and day.
Beneath the stars, the ripples dance,
In calm embrace, we find our chance.

A crescent moon, a silver gleam,
Reflects the heart, ignites a dream.
The tide pulls gently on the shore,
As secrets linger, evermore.

Upon a raft of woven dreams,
I drift away, or so it seems.
The ocean hums a soothing tune,
Beneath the vast, enchanted moon.

The breeze, like silk, caresses skin,
In quietude, the soul can win.
Each splash and sigh, a story shared,
In tranquil waters, none are scared.

So here I'll rest, and time will freeze,
In perfect peace, beneath the trees.
For in this sea, my heart's delight,
Is found in every starry night.

The Mysterious Calm of Ocean Depths

Beneath the surface, shadows play,
In silent realms where dreams decay.
The ocean holds its breath, so deep,
In mysteries, the secrets keep.

A world adorned in azure hue,
With creatures born of myths so true.
In stillness, depth begins to call,
The echoing whispers, rise and fall.

In caverns dark, where light won't reach,
The echoes of the deep beseech.
What tales are spun in depths concealed,
Of sunken ships and treasures healed?

A siren's song, a ghostly wail,
In the ocean's heart, where dreams set sail.
A tranquil calm, an endless quest,
In hidden depths, we seek our rest.

Yet here I float, on water clear,
In weightlessness, I shed my fear.
For in this calm, all strife will cease,
In ocean's hush, I find my peace.

Enigmas of the Neptune's Embrace

In Neptune's arms, the waters swirled,
A gentle tide where dreams unfurled.
The salt-kissed air, a spellbound sway,
In mystery, we drift away.

The playful waves, they tease and beckon,
With every splash, a word unspoken.
Soft whispers float on currents bold,
Revealing secrets, yet untold.

A coral palace shines below,
Where mermaids laugh and sea winds blow.
Each shell a token of a past,
In Neptune's hold, time's shadow cast.

The ocean's depths, a canvas wide,
Each stroke a tale of love and pride.
In rippling echoes, truths exchanged,
Through Neptune's kiss, our lives are changed.

As twilight paints the sea in gold,
In Neptune's realm, we find the old.
For every wave that rolls and breaks,
In every heart, the ocean wakes.

Dreaming Beneath the Surface

In twilight's hush, where shadows play,
The world above drifts far away.
Beneath the waves, in silken dreams,
A realm of wonder softly gleams.

With coral spires and whispers low,
A language only creatures know.
The echo of a siren's call,
In depth where ancient secrets sprawl.

Bubbles rise like thoughts unspoken,
A tale of love, of hearts once broken.
Where time is lost in ocean's waltz,
And every ripple holds its faults.

In this abyss, I seek and find,
The echoes of a love entwined.
Each creature dances, twirls, and sways,
In dreams where twilight fades to rays.

So dive with me in azure deep,
Where currents stir and shadows sleep.
Let worries fade, let silence reign,
In the embrace of gentle rain.

The Calm Before the Storm

The sky a canvas, painted gray,
As whispers warm the coming day.
A stillness wraps around the shore,
Where secrets linger, tales galore.

Soft tides beckon with tender grace,
Promising storms will soon embrace.
The horizon bleeds with muted light,
A dance of shadows, a fleeting sight.

The wind stirs softly, a breath, a sigh,
As seagulls circle, their shadows fly.
The thrill of change hangs in the air,
A magic woven, rich and rare.

Each heartbeat quickens, nature breathes,
As silence rustles through the leaves.
Beneath the calm, a wild heart throbs,
Anticipation, the world absorbs.

Hold tightly now, the moment gleams,
Before the chaos shatters dreams.
Let hope unfurl like sails at sea,
In that sweet breath of what will be.

A Tapestry of Seafoam Whispers

Beneath the sun, where waters gleam,
A tapestry of thoughts and dreams.
With threads of silver, spun with care,
The whispers weave through salty air.

Each wave that crashes tells a tale,
Of ships that sailed, of winds that wail.
Secrets buried in sandy beds,
Where every grain of history spreads.

With every ebb, a story flows,
Of mermaids where the seaweed grows.
In harmony, the currents stir,
With seafoam whispers, soft and pure.

The ocean hums a lullaby,
As birds take flight and spirits fly.
Together woven, night and day,
A dance of life, a bright ballet.

So listen close, let longing soar,
For seafoam secrets on the shore.
In every splash, in every crest,
The ocean sings what hearts invest.

Secrets of the Enchanted Current

In depths where magic intertwines,
The current holds its ancient signs.
With shimmering scales and glinting eyes,
The truth beneath the surface lies.

The kelp sways gently, beckoning near,
A melody only dreamers hear.
Where fish weave through like thoughts untold,
In waters warm, in currents bold.

Beneath the waves, a spark of light,
A treasure cradled out of sight.
The stories linger, old and wise,
In hidden realms where magic flies.

With every ripple, whispers call,
Of guardian spirits guarding all.
They echo softly, guiding souls,
Through underwater, hidden shoals.

So dive into the liquid air,
Where secrets swim and wonders dare.
In enchanted currents, let us roam,
For in the depths, we find our home.

The Water's Soft Embrace

In twilight's glow, the water gleams,
A silver thread of whispered dreams.
Each wave a tale, so sweet, it flows,
In its embrace, the heart well knows.

Beneath the surface, secrets dance,
A world alive in silken chance.
The gentle pull of rippling grace,
Carries the soul to a tranquil place.

With every tide, the memories wake,
Of laughter shared and vows we make.
The moonlight casts its tender light,
Upon the depths, all feels so right.

Oh, how the waters softly sing,
Of all the joy that life can bring.
In every swell, the echoes drift,
A soothing balm, a timeless gift.

Let go of fears, just close your eyes,
In this embrace, the spirit flies.
For in the currents, we shall find,
The endless love that binds mankind.

Soliloquy of Silent Ripples

In quiet moments, whispers play,
As ripples kiss the edge of day.
Each gentle sway, a thoughtful sigh,
A secret spoken, soft and nigh.

Beneath the hush, the heart must hear,
The tales of hope that linger near.
And in the flow, a dance unfolds,
Of dreams unspoken, yet retold.

The silence speaks in patterns rare,
Of love, of loss, of tender care.
Each droplet falls, a memory's thread,
Weaving the past where we once tread.

In solitude, the ripples gleam,
A tranquil pulse, a softening beam.
Embrace the sound, though faint it seems,
For life resides in whispered dreams.

With every hush, the world retreats,
In stillness found, the soul completes.
So let the water's voice be heard,
In silent ripples, every word.

Distant Shores of the Heart

On distant shores, our hearts will roam,
With tides that beckon us back home.
The sands of time, they slip away,
Yet love remains, a bright array.

As waves caress the rocky coast,
Each ebb and flow, a cherished ghost.
In azure depths, the dreams abide,
With whispered thoughts that never hide.

The horizon calls, a voice so clear,
With every heartbeat, drew you near.
And in the mist, our secrets gleam,
Across the waters, we weave our dream.

As the sun dips low, the skies ignite,
Our spirits soar, a sweet delight.
For in the distance, love's embrace,
Awaits our souls, a sacred space.

Through stormy seas and skies of grey,
The heart will find its destined way.
On distant shores, we'll meet once more,
In every wave, love's sweet rapport.

Melodies Found Within the Stillness

In twilight's hush, the music hums,
A soft refrain of gentle drums.
In every drop that falls and gleams,
A symphony of silent dreams.

The stillness holds a tender tune,
As stars awaken, light the dune.
In quietude, where echoes blend,
The heart finds peace, a timeless friend.

Listen close to nature's song,
It soothes the soul, where we belong.
With every breeze that stirs the leaves,
A melody that nature weaves.

From brook to bay, the chorus swells,
In tranquil depths, the beauty dwells.
As moonlight dances on the shore,
Each silent note invites us more.

In moments still, the heart takes flight,
A wondrous journey igniting light.
For in this peace, we find our way,
To melodies that softly play.